ISBN 979-8-9913942-4-6

Published by Hidden Hand Press
www.hiddenhandbooks.com

HIDDEN HAND PRESS

Of Spice and Stone

Hamant Singh

Contents

Part II: Molcaxitl | Creation

"I cook with wine, sometimes I even add it to the food."
-W.C. Fields

"When Allah created me, he knew that I would drink a lot of wine. So if I didn't, the omniscience of Allah would stand on its head."
- Omar Khayyám (Rubaiyat De Omar Khayyam)

PREFACE

It's hard to imagine that something as basic as food could evolve into subject matter for a book of poems and stories. Then again, I suppose there is philosophy in everything if we look for it.

Eat to Live or *Live to Eat* has been the perennial question, hasn't it? I grew up living by the former credo before I switched over to the latter. Like most that have before, there rarely is a regression. Travelling for many years opened the doors to dishes and cuisines hitherto unheard of. However, nostalgia eventually did set in, leaving me with the inevitable craving for the food I grew up with.

Almost instinctively, I began learning recipes from my mother, that came from her mother (and probably hers before that). Being in the kitchen brought about several adventures and accidents that are well-mixed into this book. Still, nothing holds my attention as much as the mortar and pestle—an ageless concept that transcends continents.

I like to think it may well have been the very beginning of the creation/destruction dialectic. The violence of these transitory phases exist in the oscillations between several spheres, in and out of the kitchen. Yet, they seem to be two sides of the same coin—solve et coagula. However, considering how often we find that 'creation' demands destruction first, perhaps it is not possible to use the term 'create' as simplistically as we do.

This book is dedicated to everyone I've dined with, drank with, cooked with and cooked for. As with all my previous books, it is hoped that this collection also finds a special place on your bookshelf and that it will be enjoyed time and time again. May your gins be cold, your spice cabinet full, and your recipes never find any peace.

PART I:
TEXOLOTL | DESTRUCTION

Note to Parents

Dear Mother and Father,

Throw your child into a *khrok*[1] as soon as their bones are hard enough to break. This usually means when they are about 2 or 3 years old. Conform and blend until incomprehensible.

Do this without mercy, for to spare the rod is to spoil the child. Please do not wash away the stains. Continue to use the *khrok* daily as a reminder of what they need and what you need.

When they are old enough to become a parent themselves, humiliate them into parenthood with the aforementioned used *khrok*. That they too, may use it well, as you have used it. That they too may conform and blend until incomprehensible.

---

[1] ครก: Thai mortar and pestle.

That it too may serve them well, as it has served you.

As Usual That Tuesday

The gifts poured over the delicate bride on her big day. She welcomed each gift with a soft embrace and a wide smile. Gentle little trinkets that were floated into her hands and then on to the *mesa de regalos*. Familiarity in family and friends although she had not seen some in years, *muy familiar*.

As the line progressed, she saw a face more familiar than the others. *Muy familiar.* Her mother's eyes rose to meet hers before they flooded with tears. In her mother's arms, was cradled the magnificent monolith that plodded with her all through her childhood.

¿Qué? ¿Su molcajete²?

Sí, mija.

---

² A mortar, in most of Mesoamerica.

A dense heirloom that bore the weight of generations and that culinary burden of wifehood. What a way to celebrate this new beginning! A gift like this?! In classic *abuelita* fashion, her mother began explaining the symbolism of the gift, adding to the weight in the process. She pointed out the symbiotic nature of the *molcajete* and the *tejolote*[3]—how one was useless without the other.

In the early months of her union, she made salsas several times a week with her mother's heavy *molcajete*. Tweaking the recipes each time, she felt fertile—giving birth to new creations each time she pounded hard in the evenings.

However, as marital bliss soon faded in little over a year, the pairing simultaneously fell into a state of mundanity and then fell out of love. Consequently, she found herself using the *molcajete* less and less frequently, as it sat in its

---

[3] A pestle, in most of Mesoamerica.

own special place in the kitchen. Cobwebs began to grow over it that trembled each time voices were raised in the house. The large rock sat there dormant like the volcano it came from. Just waiting.

~

He came home drunk as usual that Tuesday, stumbling through the front door and trailing a curious blend of whiskey and cheap perfume. With heavy legs, he plodded through the house as usual that Tuesday. Aroused by her husband's noisy entrance, a wife entered the kitchen to find him on the ground. Out of love, she started nagging as usual that Tuesday. She went on and on about how she felt neglected, how she felt like a useless burden on him. He yelled at her as usual that Tuesday to shut up, to leave him alone and that he wished he never had married her.

In a swift blend of stupor and rage, his searching hand found the nearest thing to him and he promptly flung it in the direction of his wife. As it turned out, the only thing swifter than his sludgy mind was his arm. That Tuesday, she learnt a new use for *molcajetes* that she had never even thought about before. In fact, she never thought about it since.

"So long as you have food in your mouth, you have solved all questions for the time being."
- Omar Khayyám (Rubaiyat De Omar Khayyam)

My First Molcajete

The heavy burden
Was a cruel gift—
A weapon
I cradled
In my arms.

Why did I need to cure it?
Was it sick?
Did I accept disease?
Why did they give me something
So sick?
Does this make me a *curandero*?

Here is where we fall
In love.

If you don't
Cure a *molcajete*,
You will eat stones
For months and months.

Pies para qué los quiero
Si tengo este molcajete para maldecir?

Seed I Found

As I readied it,
I noticed it
A seed
Left behind.
Who hadn't washed it,
Cleansed it,
Used it?

Was it
A grandmother,
A mother
A sister,
Whose seed was it?

How does
A senseless swallower
Receive remnants?
Does it pretend?
Does it force assimilation?

Is my mix
Mine?
Or are there crumbs
Of a previous pounding?

I'm not sure
If I should
Integrate remnants
Or start anew.

How does creation begin
If seed is not
Left behind?

"Drink wine. This is life eternal. This is all that youth will give you. It is the season for wine, roses and drunken friends. Be happy for this moment. This moment is your life."
- Omar Khayyam

"Destruction, hence, like creation, is one of Nature's mandates."
- Marquis de Sade

CHILAQUILES

At what point
Did the corn die?
Was it before
It was picked,
Was it before
It was dried?

It stopped existing
When it was
Drowned.
Then they heaped
Gravesoil on it
Until there was barely a trace.

O how the living
Continually feed
On death;
How the living
Continually resurrect
The dead.

Ashtrays

I have cigarettes
Of life with you.
But they are really
Just
Crackling embers
That die out
As soon as they are
Aflame.

With every breath
We glow
And burn out
Until there is
Nothing left.
We discard an echo
And then light
Another.

And now I find myself
With ashtrays
Full of ashed rays.

Lost in a haze,
I mindlessly reach
And set ablaze
Another fleeting memory.

Insomnia

With waking sighs,
With tired eyes,
I wander empty.
How I crave a weight
Upon these exhausted eyelids.

Powerless,
I remain
Awake
Without not having
Fully been awoken.
I dream
Of falling
Asleep,
Waking up
And facing the vast desert
Of Infinity.

That my ears
Would be flooded
With sweet silence,

That my nostrils
Would be drenched
With boisterous stench,
That my mouth
Would be filled
With fetid death.

With gesturing nod,
He motions me
In the direction of
His poison-tipped sword.

I taste
The bitter sting
Of the great serpent,
I taste
The sweet bliss
Of the Great Awakening.

Mourning Coffee

A waterfall of darkness pours forth and fills my cup. I can't tell if my eyes are filled with morning crusties or dried tears. My body is freezing in this cold, as is hers. She is no more but I am still here.

I finger the handle lightly before lifting the cup to my lips. An ephemeral warmth fills my body and dissipates before the cup reaches the table again. Between the murmurs and hushed voices, I hear the tedious repetitions. "I'm sorry," they say and go on their merry way. The words warm the tips of my earlobes and I quickly forget their emptiness.

Where will I find warmth that will stay? I find myself with an abyssal unfathomable inside me that swallows any warmth as soon as it enters. Whatever shall I fill the void with?

Each warm swig is accompanied by a fading memory—biscuit nibbles to coffee sips. Why do they call them 'the *de*-ceased' as if her ended life will return? Why can't I fathom the sort of necromancy in this word?

A green bottle catches the corner of my eye, between the well-wishers and goodbyes. I smile and nod and smile and nod as my body grows colder still. I wait for them all to leave, as they always do, before uncapping the bottle of whiskey. I sip once more, hoping to find some reprieve from this rigid frigidity.

This time, I found warmth that remained a close companion of mine till unconsciousness found me.

On Phocomelia

Your eyes, your nose,
His eyebrows,
Your sharp tongue.
That discerning whip,
That scourge
That was meant
To rule the world.
But to whom
Do these arms belong to?

Why did I inherit these?
What am I to do
With these hand-me-downs?
What good is this
Insulting *molcajete*
That I cannot use?

While wives
Moan and groan
About all the kitchen work
And house work,

I can only watch.
Unable to protest,
Unable to applaud

The efforts,
Unable to grasp
The struggle—

Unabled.

"Every act of creation is first an act of destruction."
- Pablo Picasso

"Cooking is like love. It should be entered into with abandon or not at all."
- Harriet Van Horne

KrsnaKali

O swallower of time!
Accountant of spent moons and suns!
Kal
Oscillating infinitely
Between imagined yesterdays and fabricated
tomorrows.

Obliterators of time—
Thou, agent of chaos
That crawled out
Of the clock
And broke both its hands.
Your black magnificence
Engulfs all,
Well swallowed
Into an abyss
Where form and word
Are none.

O how you possess
With your pithy vengeance!

Mother, Nurturer, Destroyer—
Secrets
That waterfall off your extended
Tongue.
How *they* call upon
You
And you render it
Irrelevant
In that spicy bliss
Of transcendence.

O divine keeper of time!
Dazzling dancer,
With a broken flute
And an untuned *damru*.
Drive this deaf hoard back
Into the black lands of oblivion!

G&T

I struggle
With your noisy bubbling sizzle,
And there you perturb
My silence.

My poison
When I am far away
From the others;
My solace
When the beer and whisky
Has run dry.

What is it
Of your sours?
What is it
Of your bitterness?
There is nothing sweet
About your kiss—
I am drinking death.

You deliver me to slumber
After the longest days
And rot
My mortality away.

And when that deathly tide
Has passed,
My bonier finger
Will beckon another.

La Cantina

Drunks buzz
Around like the flies
That wander in
For a chat.

A void
Stuck in time
Where smoking cigarettes is
Still normal.

Where problems dissolve
Into *rancheras*
And cheap beer.
We turn
Our problems
Into performances,
Our screwups
Into symphonies,
And obligations
Into orchestras.

All the while,
A row
Of empty bottles
Paraded
Like trophies
For every round
You survived.

Meanwhile,
Wives are at home
Pounding frustrations
Into a loaded *molcajete*.
Paraded
Like trophies
For every round
She survived.

"The main facts in human life are five: birth, food, sleep, love, and death."
- E.M. Forster

"I'm going to put death in all their food and watch them die."
- Shirley Jackson,
We Have Always Lived in the Castle

Pan de Muerto

I lay a loaf
On the *ofrenda⁴*,
That you might find
Sustenance
For whatever it is
You need to sustain.

I lay a loaf
On your grave
Amidst the chaos,
That you might find your way
Through the people, the *fiesta*,
The candles, the *musica*,
Back to your resting place.

To dress a loaf of bread
With edible bones
And then sugarcoat
Food for the dead.

---

⁴ A colourful altar with various offerings for the dead.

How literal,
How obvious...
Death must be bitter
And the dead must be hungry.

How wonderful
It must be
To be able to taste
In the afterlife.

PART II:
MOLCAXITL | CREATION

"Stop worrying about how your breath's going to smell, whether there's *beurre blanc* on your face, or whether ordering the braised pork belly will make you look fat. Eating with abandon couldn't be more of a turn-on: it shows that you're comfortable with yourself...

For a dinner date, I eat light all day to save room, then I go all in: I choose this meal and this order, and I choose you, the person across from me, to share it with. There's a beautiful intimacy in a meal like that. It's about exploration and taste. And kissing after dinner. And maybe there's a little wine and curry on your breath...and that's nice."

- Anthony Bourdain

Samādhi

Each thumping pound
Is a step closer
To Nirvana.
The rhythms progress,
And sounds possess—
Adults are reduced
To children
For easier digestion.

The Self is chipped away
With repetitive hammering,
Resembling a ticking clock,
Or a ticking bomb.

Not to pulverise
But to disappear.
Where entire concepts
Are reimagined
Fragments—
Scrapped traces.
Memories

Of what used to be.

And fools say
Nothing is set
In stone.
Destroy by your hand,
And create by it.

This is how
You play god.

TENET

(First published in Morsus Vitae Issue 4)

My account
Is an account
Of oscillations.
A nameless pendulum
Senselessly swinging between
Hope and memories—
A pendulum in a dark room
That heaves with sorrow.

They watch over the pendulum,
Circling and moaning.
Shackled and howling,
My ghouls tear up the silence
With cacophonous reminders
Of lies and regret,
Of maladies and deceit.

When
Did I stop living?
I know

That I had a thirsty mouth
Greedy for the infinite
Ocean of the world.
My thirsty mouth is now dry
As a bone—
The sandy mouth
Of a hungover Sunday
With a throat scarred
And parched from screaming.

Nasi Kangkang,
or How We Fell in Love

To feed her desires,
She seeks refuge in
Inferior gnosis—
To blind him,
To shackle him,
Enslave him
And engrave him.

Elevated,
She hovers
Over the offering
As vapours
Liquify her quim—
The honey pot
Drizzling dribbles
Into a rice pot.

A secret secretion
Rains over the grains

While tragic magic
Reigns over rice.
Pouring pestilence
Into sustenance,
She shackles his will
As the fool eats his fill.

She pulls the wool
Over his eyes
Then drowns his soul
With poisonous lies.

An eventual reprieve arrives—
A horrific abrupt demise.
The only real love here
Is the one he had for rice.

"I feel like I've been hungover for half my life."

- Ruth Hall

ARROZ

ARROZ

Recipe for Disaster
(or: Sambal Belacan)

- 5 red chillies, or *chile serrano*
- 5 *cili padi*, or *cabe rawit*, or *cabe gendot* (*habanero jangan[5]*); or just use 5 more of the above
- Juice of one lime or one *calamansi*
- Thumbnail sized chunk of *belacan, terasi, ngapi* or *kapi[6]*. A bit more if you appreciate these unique flavours
- Salt, as much as needed
- One or two Kaffir lime leaves

Begin the ritual by surrendering all your chillies into a *molcajete, ulekan* or *batu lesung[7]*. Channel all your anger, frustration and hatred from the pestle to the chillies. Be mindful of possible karmic backlash onto your face or into your

---

[5] Malay for "don't".
[6] Various names for shrimp paste in different Southeast Asian languages.
[7] Various names for mortar and pestles.

eyes. This will take all the joy out of hunger and you will feel the full burn of ancestral venom. Continue to do this until you reach a near-Nirvana state of satisfaction.

Pass your *belachan* piece through fire, cleansing it of its oceanic memories. Add it into the mix. At this stage, you typically should not need much more violence.

Continue to combine the resultant chaotic mess with your citric secretions and salt. Mix well, overturning from the bottom—for this is where most revolutions begin.

Garnish with the sweet-smelling aforementioned leaves broken in twain.

Congratulations!
You now have pure bliss—flavour independent of tradition and identity bullshit.

The only challenge that truly remains is if you can put this reduction in your mouth and survive. Tears and heartburn are normal but are not at all necessary.

Reduction

Take my tales
And pulverize them.
Chasing tails
And heartache,
As moments dissolve into
Fragments.

Take my tears
For they lubricate
The gears—
Gasoline
For the great machine.

Take my smiles
For they are nobody.
Temporary sanctuary
That is brief reprieve,
Before they disappear
And sorrow resumes
Her melancholic song.

Take the advice
And throw it out
Like soiled hand-me-downs.
Irrelevant—
Since they are not,
You?

Take and take
And take some more
Till nothing remains
But scraps.

All that is left
Is a nameless ghost
Rummaging through messy mush
With grinder in hand,
Searching for bliss
At the bottom
Of a receptacle.

"When one burns one's bridges,
what a very nice fire it makes."
- Dylan Thomas

The English countryside, its growth and its
destruction, is a genuine and tragic theme.
- E. M. Forster

"The body politic, as well as the human body,
begins to die as soon as it is born, and carries itself
the causes of its destruction."
- Jean-Jacques Rousseau

Mother's Recipes

(for Nimmi John, the first true woman I have
ever known)

Did you watch and make note,
Or were they handed to you
In a book that was
Bound?
Did you get the chance to earn
The amount of salt
That goes into the blend?

Salt
Will make or break
Any plan
Known
To Man.

Do you
Turn to recipes
After ten attempts
At the same?

The same—
Or have formulas been phased out
By deft movements
Of your skilled hand?

Perhaps, her recipes have become
Irrelevant.
Perhaps, your mother too.

For these rules were
Perfect
For *her* tongue,
Your mother
And her recipes.

Tell me,
Did your father
Leave you
Any?

Cloudeater

I look at you
Stain the sky
And wonder
What you would taste like.

Would you taste
Of dreams?
Of imagination—
Pagination
Floating in stasis.

Would you taste
Of memories?
Bittersweet cotton candy
Wafting between
This plane and
The Otherside.

Would you taste
Of sunlight—
Those temporary

Rays that make me see?

I see you
And know
That when I reach you,
You are nothingness.

I am the Cloudeater
And I will devour
Everything
Between Now and Then,
And Later.

Chocolate

You chew a square
In your mouth,
I do not.

I keep it there
So that it melts away,
So that I can transcend,
So that I understand.

I keep it there
So that my tongue is sweet,
So that I cannot speak,
So that you cannot understand.

Keep it there
So that it disappears,
So that *I* disappear,
So that writing appears,
So that you may understand.

Keep chewing squares
In your mouth,
I will not.

"To eat is to appropriate by destruction."
- Jean-Paul Sartre

"Wine is bottled poetry."
- Robert Louis Stevenson

Out with the New,
In with the Old

Because you need to earn your dinner.
Because it's all about the grind
Because the lazy way out never quite satisfies.
Because your husband gave you a rock
Because your mother gave you a rock
Because *her* mother gave it to her.
Because grinding is not blending.

Because you never begin a sentence with
Just because.
Because a *molcajete* has endured a trial by fire.
Because blenders just don't cut it
Because oils need to be extracted
Because the concept is eternal and universal.

Because
To argue about it only causes us to fall into the pit
of Because,

And there we shall perish with the dogs of Reason.[8]

Of Garlic and Other Wards

Warn your wards
That garlic keeps
The undead
At bay.
This is what the afterlife must be—
Layered white bitter husks
With a pungent
Biting spice.

Where a skewer
Of garlic, onion and chilli
Keeps the rains at bay—
A stick askew
Of garlic and other wards,
In other words.

While a Catholic priest
Heaps salt in corners,
Thirsty demons watch,
Parched
For human blood.

This is why
Bloodthirsty
Fanged creatures
Do not exist in Asian
Folklore.

O how it is a wonder
That sweet cinnamon
Keeps the ants away.

The Uninvited Guest

(for Beliaya'al)

A cold night's sup 'twixt man and wife,
An unmarked chair that's full of strife.
A third did sit with no invite,
A dark nocturnal parasite.

O King of Hell! I know those eyes!
I know that smile, that tongue of knives.
This table feeds the hungry man!
A bounteous spread by my wife's hand.

The smiling guest with breath so foul
Did grace a home with feral growl.
He ate his fill and bones were crunched,
Yet not a morsel there was munched.

By light of fire, I watched him feast—
She disappeared into the beast.
My wife was now no more to be

And then with glee, he turned to me.

He ate my joy and drank my tears
And all my memories for years.
In deafening inquietude,
On both our souls he gnawed and chewed.

His deafened ears heard no reprieve,
This unplanned stay was all but brief.
For years and years, I roamed the land
I walked on feet but not as man.

Liminal Spaces

Can you hear the agonising hunger
Of an empty *khrok*?
Its growling emptiness,
Purposelessness—
The need to be filled.

Can you hear the anguished cries
Of a kitchen knife?
Laying dormant
In a drawer,
A growing thirst,
Purposeless
Without a vegetable
To tear through.

The piercing ironies
Seem to slice
Through dormancy—
Charged potential,
Boiling.
Not at all different

From a volcano
Waiting to erupt.
Do we curse the fate
We seemingly exist for
Or should we begin
To invent new destinies
For ourselves?

ABOUT THE AUTHOR

HAMANT SINGH is a Singaporean writer who is inspired by the Sublime in horror, different cultures and the occult. *Of Spice and Stone* is his sixth release after *The Sibyl* (2002), *CHAOS: RRR* (2023), *NÁUSEA / CONFESIÓN* (2023), *VALTOHA* (2024) and *Andromeda Dreams* (2024). After a poem was nominated for the 2022 Rhysling Award by the Science Fiction Poetry Association, *The Sibyl* was listed on the preliminary ballot for the 2023 Bram Stoker Awards (Superior Achievement in a Poetry Collection). In 2023, *The Sibyl* was also nominated for the Elgin Award.

Hamant currently resides in Guadalajara, Mexico where he is currently working on an art/poetry collaboration with Irish artist Shane Reilly among several other different projects.

www.ingramcontent.com/pod-product-compliance
Lightning Source LLC
Chambersburg PA
CBHW051642120626
46551CB00015B/2190